Lypptuss the Gum Tree Dragon

You Too Can Have Friends

Grace Kennedy
Dwayne Kennedy

Dr Dee Books

Publication

Published by Dr Dee Books
An Imprint of Ability Therapy Specialists Pty Ltd
PO Box 4065, Armidale, New South Wales, Australia 2350
ISBN: 978-1-925034-17-2 [Hardcover]

Keywords: Children, Youth, Adult, Story, Tale, Dragon, Myth, Legend, Artwork, Indigenous, Aboriginal, First Nation, Australian, Canadian, Birthday, Friendship, Friend, Loneliness, Solitude, Social Isolation, Sadness, Depression, Stress, Anxiety, Healing

Reading Level: This book is produced for primary school levels one to six.

About this Book

Lypptuss the Gum Tree Dragon: You Too Can Have Friends, is a heartwarming story for hearts young and not so young. A beautiful family treasure, this book is based on a long-protected and thirty-year-old manuscript. The drawings had showed a lovely yellow patina as a loving sign of age, timelessness, and beauty. Digitally reproduced and enhanced, the original artwork is by Dwayne and complements the story written by Grace many years ago. It was her dream to see this work shared with others. Joseph provided editing, layout, design, and contributions to the text.

About the Authors

Grace Kennedy is a mother, grandmother, and great grandmother. Dwayne Kennedy is a Counsellor and an Early Childhood Specialist. Joseph Bowers is a Psychotherapist and Behaviour Specialist.

Dedication

Jo-Anna Mary

About Lypptuss

Named after the Eucalyptus Gum Tree, 'Lypptuss' is one very special and mystical dragon who comes to children young and not so young in the Dreamtime of Life. A Healing Dragon, Lypptuss can be found where emotions are at the surface, and people are trying to be their best. She is, at heart, very kind and beautiful. This is her very first ever book. She is so amazingly excited to share this special day with you… Her first ever Birthday.

ONCE UPON A TIME
There was a DRAGON named LYPPTUSS.

This was a very special day.
It was Lypptuss' BIRTHDAY!

But Lypptuss had NOT ONE FRIEND in all the world.
She was feeling very lonely.

She said to herself,
"Today, I am going to find myself a FRIEND!"

Lypptuss was a GOOD DRAGON.
But she was a very UGLY dragon too!

Or so, she had been told…

On this SPECIAL DAY
Lypptuss decided to wander in the bush…

The first creatures she came to
Were TWO TADPOLES and a FROG.

She asked, "Will you PLEASE be my friends?"

The two tadpoles, and the frog remained SILENT...

They just looked at Lypptuss
Like she had the most UGLY head!

Lypptuss said, "Today is my birthday!"

The tadpoles and the frog said with one loud voice,
"No way! You are just too BIG and too UGLY!"

Lypptuss walked away very SAD...

Then a GOOD THOUGHT came into her mind…
"I wonder what FRIEND we can find?"
Lypptuss then trotted off again, feeling much better

She came to a MIGHTY GUM TREE.
With branches stretching as far as you can see!
Guess who she saw?! Can you find him?

Yes!!! A Wise Koala Bear in an Old Gum Tree!
Lypptuss was very hope filled in her heart.

She asked, "Dear Wise Koala, will you be my FRIEND?
For today is my BIRTHDAY!"

"No way!" Said Koala. "You are just too UGLY! Go away!"
Now Lypptuss felt very, very SAD… So, she trotted away…

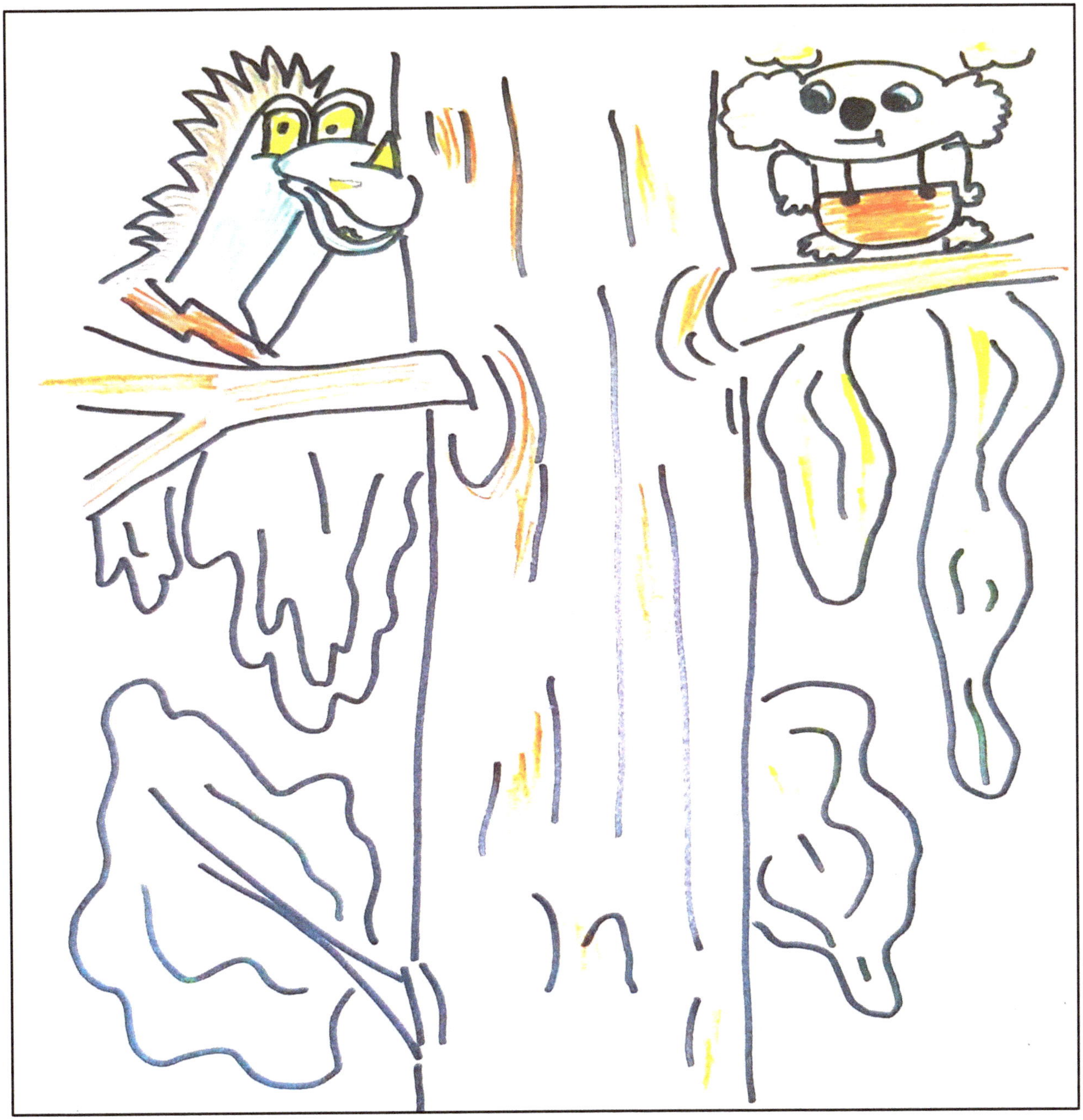

Next, poor sad Lypptuss met a very BIG bird…
A rather huge BIRD, you ever did see.
Oh me, Oh my, how absurd can this be?

Feeling uncertain, afraid, and lonely,
And most certainly not FREE…
Lypptuss the Lonely Dragon stuttered these words,
"Please be my FRIEND, Dear Pelican Sir Bird.
Today is my BIRTHDAY, and not a friend we can find."

"No, no." Said Sir Pelican, "Most grave, most dire.
To be without Friend or Fire in the heart.
Even on your birthday, how sad, how forlorn.
But No, No, No!
I cannot be a FRIEND to a BIG UGLY DRAGON
You must think me mad, or a tad bit not smart."

So, yet again, our secret most friend, a beauty nonetheless,
But no one could be told. She was so, so sad.
And like the Star of her name, kept trying, kept trying,
Though no one was buying.

Then from a GUM TREE FOREST
Came a Little Freddy Mouse.
Happily, left his house, Freddy Mouse
Sat on an Old Tree Stump.

"Mr. Fred the Mouse, Sir…
Today is my BIRTHDAY, will you be my FRIEND?"

"Simply No, No, No!
Chirped the mouse, you have no cheese!
And no BEAUTY to be behold…
Or so I have been told…
Go away before I change my mind.
For no UGLIER DRAGON can we find."

Completely saddened like a wet old towel,
Lypptuss the GUM TREE Dragon
Rested for a moment, no energy to fly, trot, or run…

Then a GOOD THOUGHT came into mind…
"If no one is around, and no friend to find,
Then I will WISH up a good soul of my OWN KIND…

So Lypptuss found a most beautiful wishing well
Of water so pure, so clean, and refreshing.
"Let me speak these magic words," she said.
"Let me sing, let me dance!
To this Water Well, let these words be my spell.
A FRIEND I SEE, A FRIEND TO BE…"

She CLOSED her eyes oh so tight…
She PULLED in her long arms and tail…
She wished, and wished, and WISHED to take flight…
Until her EYEBALLS were near to fail…

Then peeking with just one eye open,
Lypptuss looked down into the Water.
Nothing much she could see… But a wiggle, a wobble.
She signed a deep sadness, "Even my wishes don't reap.
Not even myself wants to be FRIEND to me!"

Still sad, still feeling down, Lypptuss the Dragon
Perched beside a BILLABONG
And she cried many tears, howled and sighed…
Sobbing, and crying, and so lonely inside.

"Well…" She said, "I best be going home now."
She thought in her mind, "No FRIEND, not even ONE."
Then looking up, "Only the GUM TREES sing today.
This will make me seek to stop this sorry weep…"

Holding up her head, she turned once, then again,
And once more! She turned, and turned, and churned
Out a BIG CIRCLE.

LYPPTUSS flapped her wings and wagged her tail.
"This is my PRIVATE BIRTHDAY.
No matter the trail of so many 'no, no, no's'
Oh, and what terrible travail..."

Then alone but holding her head high, she said,
"I guess I am TOO BIG, TOO UGLY, for sure."

Just then, as she WALKED with heavy steps, slow and sad,
Lypptuss TURNED a corner toward home.
Strange sounds she could hear, from afar, or were they near?
Right there, right then,
Lypptuss stopped short.

"Oh, my goodness.
What be that???
Can this be???
At all be true???
Or is the Wishing Well
Giving me a trick, or three, or two?"

For there before her BIG UGLY EYES
Were ALL and EVERY and MOST and MORE
GATHERED around a ONE HUGE CAKE
And that be REAL. That's for SURE.

Frog,
Tadpoles,
Mouse,
Pelican,
Koala,
And the Old Gum Tree.
Believe me or not.
Up to you.
But it be true.

Lypptuss the GUM TREE DRAGON
Licked her chops,
Smiled the BIGGEST SMILE and CLEVER.
"My FRIENDS," she said.
"This is the BEST BIRTHDAY EVER."

Then they all SANG together,
"Happy Birthday to you. Happy Birthday to you.
Happy Birthday Dear Lypptuss. Happy Birthday to you!"

The moral of this story, let me guess?
Let me say?
Is no matter how big, small, ugly, or fair;
You have a BEAUTY at play.

You are a beasty, a DRAGON, come what may.
And no one in this world can turn you away
From the wealth, magic, and power inside.
From your self's most self you cannot hide.

Remember the water hole, the well, the lake.
Remember to drink of water, as many tears you make.

CELEBRATE your SMILE and your HEART.

One day we will all be FRIENDS, mates, and not to part.
Yes, this is true blue. Our future. Our fate.

This is Lypptuss Dragon Dreaming.

www.ingramcontent.com/pod-product-compliance
Lightning Source LLC
Chambersburg PA
CBHW061226150426
42812CB00054BA/2526

"TRANSFORMING LIVES ONE MEAL AT A TIME"

HEALING
Plates

RECIPES FOR FORGIVENESS & WELLNESS

DR. NORMA MCLAUCHLIN
DR. J. MICHELLE VANN

Dedication

To all the hearts seeking healing and the families striving to grow closer. May this book be a gentle reminder that the table is a place for connection, forgiveness, and shared love. May each recipe bring you warmth, inspire understanding, and pull you closer to those who matter most.

ISBNs:

HARDBACK - ISBN: 978-1-952315-88-6

PAPERBACK - ISBN: 978-1-952315-97-8

31-Days Wellness & Spiritual Growth Journal
Categories:
Self-Help / Journaling
- Religion / Spirituality
- Health & Wellness / Caregiving

Book Design by: Joyce Licorish - DreamEmpire Publishing
Published by:

FORGIVENESSACROSS
BORDERS

To order additional copies of the resource, write customer service:
1420 Hoke Loop Road
Fayetteville, NC 28314
FAX orders to 910-868-3300
Phone orders to 910-818-6652

Printed in the United States of America
10 9 8 7 6 5 4 3 2 1
Front cover image by Joyce Licorish - DreamEmpire Publishing
Book design by Joyce Licorish - DreamEmpire Publishing
Printed by - Amazon | Ingram Spark
First printing edition September 2024

For Author Appearances or Bookings visit:
www.ChosePen.com
contact@chosepen.com
910.758.1811

HEALING *Plates*

RECIPES FOR FORGIVENESS & WELLNESS

"TRANSFORMING LIVES ONE MEAL AT A TIME"

HEALING *Plates*

RECIPES FOR FORGIVENESS & WELLNESS

"Food is symbolic of *love* when words are inadequate."
— Alan D. Wolfelt

REVIEWS

Roy Williams, Nutritionist

★ ★ ★ ★ ★

"Healing Plates perfectly marries nutrition and emotional wellness. The focus on wholesome ingredients combined with the theme of forgiveness creates a unique approach to cooking that is both enriching and fulfilling. A must-read for anyone looking to enhance their relationship with food and others."

Emily Johnson, Wellness Advocate

★ ★ ★ ★ ★

"Healing Plates is more than a cookbook; it's a guide to nurturing your spirit through food. Each recipe is thoughtfully crafted with heartfelt stories that resonate deeply. This book has inspired me to create meaningful connections with my family and friends through shared meals."

Michael Torres, Family Therapist

★ ★ ★ ★ ★

"Dr. McLauchlin's Healing Plates beautifully illustrates the profound connection between food and emotional healing. As a therapist, I often underscore the importance of shared experiences in fostering empathy and connection. This book serves as a practical yet soulful resource in that journey."

Samantha Ellis, Culinary Blogger

★ ★ ★ ★ ★

"Every page of Healing Plates feels like a warm hug. The recipes are simple yet packed with flavor, and the personal stories accompanying them allow you to journey alongside the author. You won't just be cooking; you'll be cultivating relationships and healing."

Roy Williams, Nutritionist

★ ★ ★ ★ ★

"Healing Plates perfectly marries nutrition and emotional wellness. The focus on wholesome ingredients combined with the theme of forgiveness creates a unique approach to cooking that is both enriching and fulfilling. A must-read for anyone looking to enhance their relationship with food and others."

Prologue

In today's whirlwind of busyness and uncertainty, forgiveness can feel like an overwhelming task, yet it remains one of life's most profound gifts. Forgiveness is not just a fleeting moment or a word we say—it's a powerful transformation that begins deep within us, reshaping how we relate to ourselves and to others.

On my personal path to healing, I found that food held a remarkable ability to connect, comfort, and heal. Every meal became a chance to share, a moment to extend grace, and an opportunity to mend relationships. These were not just recipes for the body, but for the soul—nourishment that invites us to release our burdens and welcome a brighter, more fulfilling future.

Healing Plates: Recipes for Wellness and Forgiveness was born from this understanding. It's more than a collection of recipes—it's a celebration of the healing power of food. Each dish is woven with stories and reflections, offering not just sustenance but also an invitation to explore forgiveness, understanding, and love. Let's embark on this journey together, savoring each meal as a step toward wholeness, and discovering the joy of connecting through the simple yet transformative act of sharing food.

Preface

As the founder and CEO of Chosen Pen Publishing, I have always believed in the power of storytelling to connect us across different walks of life. Healing Plates: Recipes for Forgiveness and Wellness comes from a deeply personal place—reflecting my own journey toward forgiveness and my desire to create a space where food becomes a pathway to healing.

Meals are more than sustenance; they are experiences that shape our narratives and foster connection. With each recipe, I aim to evoke love, compassion, and resilience, inviting you to embrace them as steps on your own healing journey.

Let the stories touch your heart, the flavors inspire your cooking, and the reflections guide you toward forgiveness. May this collection remind you that every meal has the potential to transform lives—one plate at a time.

-Dr. Norma McLauchlin

Notes from the Author

Dear Reader,

Thank you for choosing Healing Plates: Recipes for Forgiveness and Wellness. It is my hope that this book becomes a companion on your journey toward understanding, healing, and nurturing relationships—both with yourself and others.

The inspiration for these recipes came from my personal experiences, as well as stories from those around me—family, friends, and others whose paths have intersected with mine. Each dish holds a deeper meaning, a reflection of how forgiveness and connection can start in the simplest of places—our kitchens.

As you cook, I encourage you to slow down and truly engage with the process. Let each recipe be a moment of mindfulness, and consider sharing these meals with loved ones, using them as an opportunity to foster conversation and connection.

Throughout this book, you'll find space for reflection. I encourage you to take time to sit with your thoughts after each recipe, letting the act of cooking become a meditative journey toward self-compassion, understanding, and peace. Thank you for letting this book be part of your journey. May each plate bring you closer to wellness, forgiveness, and the joy of shared meals.

With gratitude,

Dr. Norma McLauchlin, MS, MBA, EdD
Founder/CEO, Chosen Pen Publishing

Notes from the Author

Dear Reader,

Thank you for choosing Healing Plates. As a holistic wellness coach, I've seen how powerful the intersection of forgiveness and wellness can be for mind, body, and spirit healing. Healing Plates is more than a collection of recipes; it's a journey to release burdens and nourish every part of yourself.

In these pages, you'll find simple, nutritious recipes paired with reflections on forgiveness—a crucial step in shedding the weight from both our minds and bodies. Let each meal and moment remind you of your strength and the beauty of fresh starts.

May this book inspire you to embrace a lighter, more connected life.

With love and gratitude,

Dr. J. Michelle Vann, Dcc, ThD, MS
Vanntastic Solutions

Introduction

In a world often filled with disconnection, Healing Plates: Recipes for Forgiveness and Wellness offers a unique blend of nourishing recipes and heartfelt stories that guide you toward healing and forgiveness. Dr. Norma McLauchlin intertwines the art of cooking with the profound act of letting go, reminding us that the kitchen can be a sanctuary for both the body and soul.

Through this collection, you'll discover how food can be a catalyst for connection and reflection. Each recipe is an opportunity to mend hearts, strengthen relationships, and find joy in the shared experience of a meal. Let Healing Palates inspire you to embrace the transformative power of food and the deeper connections it can foster.

Eat, Sip, Heal

Welcome to Healing Plates: Recipes for Wellness and Forgiveness, a culinary journey designed not only to nourish your body but also to heal your heart. In today's fast-paced world, we often forget the importance of taking a moment to pause, reflect, and reconnect—both with ourselves and with those we love. This book is an invitation to explore how the act of cooking and sharing meals can serve as a powerful means of fostering healing and cultivating forgiveness.

Food has an extraordinary ability to bring people together. A shared meal can ignite laughter, dissolve tension, and create lasting memories. But forgiveness, too, often begins in the kitchen. Each recipe in this collection is infused with personal stories and reflections that highlight the significance of forgiveness in our lives. As we chop, stir, and simmer, we are not merely preparing food; we are nurturing relationships, promoting personal growth, and engaging in the process of letting go.

The concept of healing through food is deeply personal to me. Through my own life experiences, I have learned that the kitchen can be a sacred space—a sanctuary where we can heal old wounds and foster new beginnings. Whether you are navigating your own journey of forgiveness or simply seeking ways to enhance your wellness, I hope you find inspiration within these pages. From comforting appetizers to invigorating drinks, each recipe is designed to resonate with your heart and soul.

As you explore the recipes, I encourage you to embrace the accompanying reflections—spaces for introspection that can deepen your understanding of forgiveness and the importance of nurturing our connections with others. Each meal is an opportunity to celebrate compassion, gratitude, and resilience. Together, let's recognize that our experiences—whether sweet or bitter—are vital ingredients to the rich tapestry of life.

May the dishes crafted in your kitchen inspire lightness of heart, spark meaningful conversations, and strengthen the bonds you share with those around you. Let this book be a trusted companion on your journey toward forgiveness, wellness, and a deeper appreciation for the power of meals shared with love.

Welcome to the table, and happy cooking!

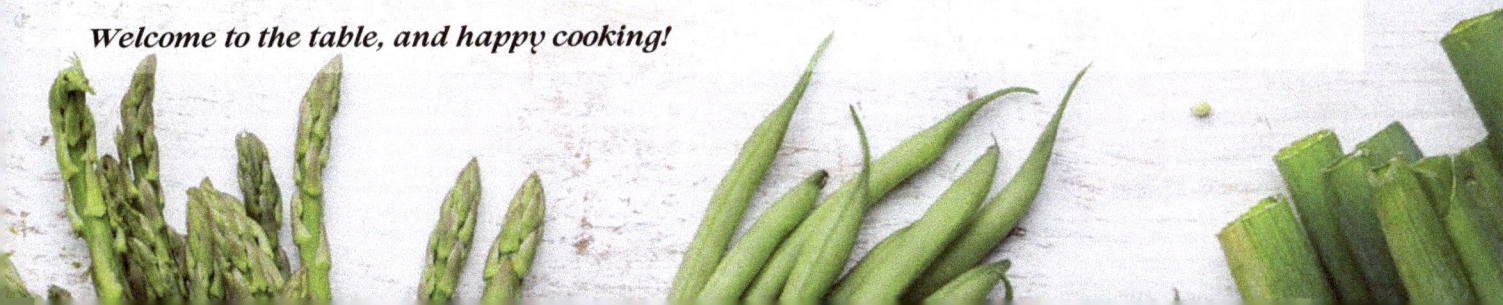

FORGIVENESS
Appetizers

"Appetizers are the little things you keep
eating until you lose your appetite."
— Joe Moore

Significance to Wellness

This bruschetta encourages letting go of past grievances and embracing the present. The act of sharing this dish fosters connection, highlighting the importance of community in the healing journey.

Letting Go Bruschetta

Personal Story

Every summer, my grandmother would host family gatherings filled with laughter and stories. Her famous bruschetta was a staple, served with an invitation to let go of past grievances and focus on the joy of the present. It reminds me that food can act as a bridge to forgiveness.

Ingredients

- 4 ripe tomatoes, diced
- 1/4 cup fresh basil, chopped
- 2 tablespoons olive oil
- 1 tablespoon balsamic vinegar
- Salt and pepper to taste
- 1 baguette, sliced and toasted

Instructions:

1. In a bowl, combine diced tomatoes, basil, olive oil, and balsamic vinegar.
2. Season with salt and pepper.
3. Toast baguette slices in the oven until golden brown.
4. Top the baguette slices with the tomato mixture just before serving.

Presentation/Table Setup & Decor

- Serve on a rustic wooden board with a few whole cherry tomatoes for garnish.
- Use a simple tablecloth with fresh herbs in small pots as centerpieces to symbolize growth.
- Provide tongs for easy picking and a large serving spoon.

Place Settings:

- Use rustic, mismatched plates to promote a cozy family gathering atmosphere.

Inner Reflection

1. What do I need to let go of to foster healthier relationships?

2. How does sharing food support my healing process?

3. Reflect on a family gathering that transformed your perspective on forgiveness.

"I release what no longer serves me, nourishing my spirit with love and harmony, as I find strength in forgiveness and the bonds that heal."

Picture Perfect

Add a photo of your prepared dish here and the people you shared it with!

Significance to forgiveness

This dish embodies the harmony found in forgiveness. The sweetness of honey juxtaposed with creamy ricotta reflects the gentle nature of compassion that enhances our relationships.

Compassion Crostini

Personal Story

I still remember the first time I made crostini for my best friend's birthday. As we shared the creamy ricotta topped with figs, we reflected on our journeys of forgiveness that brought us closer over the years.

Ingredients
- 1 cup ricotta cheese
- 2 tablespoons honey
- 4 large figs, sliced
- 1 French baguette, sliced and toasted
-

Instructions:
1. Toast slices of baguette until golden brown.
2. Spread a generous layer of ricotta cheese on each toast.
3. Drizzle with honey and top with fig slices.

Presentation Items:
Arrange beautifully on a platter, ensuring the figs are visible.

Table Setup and Decor:
Use white plates and golden utensils to enhance elegance.

Serving Utensils:
A small butter knife for spreading the ricotta.

Place Settings:
Crisp white napkins folded elegantly beside each plate.

Inner Reflection

1. When have I shown compassion to someone who needed it?

2. What discussions around food have brought healing to my relationships?

3. What can I do to demonstrate sweetness in my interactions moving forward?

Mantra

" I lead with compassion, heal through shared moments, and bring sweetness to every interaction. I am a beacon of forgiveness. "

Picture Perfect

Add a photo of your prepared dish here and the people you shared it with!

Significance to Wellness

Stuffed mushrooms are symbolic of emotional nourishment, encouraging us to fill our lives and relationships with love and warmth. They're a reminder that, like mushrooms, we thrive better in supportive environments.

Heartfelt Stuffed Mushrooms

Personal Story

Stuffed mushrooms recall warm family dinners, where sharing stories and hearty recipes transcended challenges. I learned that just like mushrooms, we can be filled with love, compassion, and understanding.

Ingredients
- 12 large portobello mushrooms
- 1 cup cream cheese
- 1/2 cup breadcrumbs
- 1/4 cup grated Parmesan cheese
- 2 cloves garlic, minced
- 1/4 cup parsley, chopped
- Salt and pepper to taste

Instructions:
1. Preheat the oven to 375°F (190°C).
2. Remove the stems from the mushrooms and chop them.
3. In a bowl, mix cream cheese, chopped stems, breadcrumbs, Parmesan cheese, garlic, and parsley. Season with salt and pepper.
4. Stuff the mixture into the mushroom caps and place them on a baking tray.
5. Bake for 20-25 minutes until golden.

Presentation Items:
Serve on a slate platter garnished with extra parsley.

Serving Utensils:
A large spoon for serving.

Place Settings:
Earth-toned plates to reflect natural colors.

Inner Reflection

1. What do I need to fill my life with to support my wellness journey?

2. How can I ensure my relationships are a source of nourishment rather than depletion?

3. Describe a time when vulnerability deepened a connection for you.

Picture Perfect

Add a photo of your prepared dish here and the people you shared it with!

Appetizers

Significance to forgiveness

Deviled eggs represent the importance of embracing change as they transform through the cooking process. They remind us that change can lead to delicious outcomes in life as well.

Embracing Change Deviled Eggs

Personal Story

Deviled eggs have been a family favorite for generations. I remember my mother making them during holiday gatherings, emphasizing that change is an essential aspect of growth in our relationships and ourselves.

Ingredients

- 6 large eggs
- 1/4 cup mayonnaise
- 1 teaspoon mustard
- Salt and pepper to taste
- Paprika for garnish

Instructions:

1. Hard boil eggs, then cool and peel.
2. Cut the eggs in half and scoop the yolks into a bowl.
3. Mix yolks with mayonnaise, mustard, salt, and pepper.
4. Refill egg whites with the yolk mixture and sprinkle with paprika.

Presentation Items

Arrange on a decorative platter for visual appeal.

Table Setup and Decor

Use pastel-colored napkins and plates for a light-hearted look.

Serving Utensils

A small ladle for filling and grabbing eggs.

Place Settings

Use colorful plates and cheerful utensils.

Inner Reflection

1. How do I view change within my relationships?

2. What changes have ultimately led to positive outcomes in my life?

3. Reflect on a time you embraced change and reaped the rewards.

" I welcome change as a path to growth, embracing its power to bring positive outcomes and deeper connections."

Picture Perfect

Add a photo of your prepared dish here and the people you shared it with!

Significance to forgiveness

Caprese skewers embody the harmony found in forgiveness, with each ingredient representing connection—tomatoes for love, mozzarella for embrace, and basil for peace. Together, they remind us of the beauty in unity.

Unity Caprese Skewers

Personal Story

The first time I prepared caprese skewers for a family reunion, the smiles on everyone's faces reminded me of how simple ingredients can unite people—just as forgiveness can reunite shaken bonds.

Ingredients

- 1 pint cherry tomatoes
- 1 pound mozzarella balls
- Fresh basil leaves
- Balsamic reduction for drizzling
- Salt and pepper to taste

How to Make

1. On a skewer, thread a cherry tomato, a basil leaf, and a mozzarella ball.
2. Repeat until the skewer is filled.
3. Drizzle with balsamic reduction and sprinkle with salt and pepper before serving.

Presentation Items

Arrange skewers on a large platter in alternating patterns for aesthetic appeal.

Table Setup and Decor

A mid-century modern table setup with clean lines and fresh flowers in a vase.

Serving Utensils

A pair of tongs or a flat serving platter for easy picking.

Place Settings

Simple white plates to highlight the colorful skewers.

Inner Reflection

1. How do various ingredients in my life come together to create harmony?

2. Reflect on an experience where different elements united for a greater good.

3. Describe a relationship that has become stronger through forgiveness.

Picture Perfect

Add a photo of your prepared dish here and the people you shared it with!

FORGIVENESS
Breakfast

"Each sunrise brings the gift of a fresh start, and with every breakfast, the chance to nourish both body and soul. Forgiveness, like the first meal of the day, is the key to beginning anew."

-Joyce Licorish

Breakfast

Significance to forgiveness

This oatmeal bowl represents comfort and nurturing. The warmth of oats reflects the importance of forgiving oneself and others to create inner peace.

Compassion Oatmeal Bowl

— Personal Story

On chilly mornings, my mother would make hearty oatmeal, filling the kitchen with warmth. Each spoonful felt like a hug, teaching me about nourishment—not just of the body but of the soul, especially during difficult times.

Ingredients

- **1 cup rolled oats**
- **2 cups almond milk**
- **1 banana, sliced**
- **1 teaspoon cinnamon**
- **2 tablespoons nut butter**

How to Make

1. In a saucepan, combine oats and almond milk and bring to a boil.
2. Reduce heat and let simmer until thick, stirring occasionally.
3. Top with sliced banana, cinnamon, and a dollop of nut butter.

Presentation Items

Serve in deep bowls with an artistic swirl of nut butter on top.

Table Setup and Decor

Use warm tones for tablecloth and placement, with candles for a cozy feel.

Serving Utensils

A large serving spoon for dishing out the oatmeal.

Place Settings

Use matching bowls and mugs for a cohesive look.

Inner Reflection

1. How does comfort food impact my emotional well-being?

2. What actions nurture my relationships?

3. Reflect on a moment when simple nourishment led to a revelation.

Mantra

❝ I embrace the comfort that nourishes my soul, nurture my relationships with intentional care, and find wisdom in the simplicity of shared moments, allowing forgiveness to bring healing and peace. ❞

Picture Perfect

Add a photo of your prepared dish here and the people you shared it with!

Breakfast

Significance to forgiveness

This smoothie indicates growth and renewal, symbolizing the healing process in forgiveness and reminding us that we can blend our experiences into a cohesive whole.

Forgiveness Smoothie

Personal Story

On days where I want something soothing to drink and find myself a tad hungry, I love making this easy recipe to start my day off light, bright, and healthy.

Ingredients
- 1 cup spinach
- 1 banana
- 1 cup almond milk
- 1/2 cup Greek yogurt
- 1 tablespoon honey

How to Make
1. In a blender, combine spinach, banana, almond milk, Greek yogurt, and honey.
2. Blend until smooth and creamy.

Presentation Items
Serve in a bright glass with a fun straw.

Preparation Needs:
A blender for mixing and a large spoon for pouring.

Garnishes:
Feel free to top it off with a banana or strawberry for good measure.

Inner Reflection

1. How can I incorporate renewal into my life?

2. Reflect on blending different aspects of your life harmoniously.

3. Describe a moment when you experienced growth after forgiveness.

Mantra

❝ I welcome renewal into every aspect of my life, blend its diverse elements into harmony, and embrace profound growth through the healing power of forgiveness. ❞

Picture Perfect

Add a photo of your prepared dish here and the people you shared it with!

Breakfast

Significance to forgiveness

This smoothie indicates growth and renewal, symbolizing the healing process in forgiveness and reminding us that we can blend our experiences into a cohesive whole.

Harmony Breakfast Parfait

Personal Story

Creating breakfast parfaits with my children taught me the value of layering experiences—how the delightful combinations of flavors can tell a story of togetherness and acceptance. Each bite was a reminder of how we support one another in our journeys.

Ingredients

- 2 cups Greek yogurt
- 1 cup granola
- 1 cup mixed berries
- Honey for drizzling

How to Make

1. In a glass, layer Greek yogurt, granola, and mixed berries.
2. Repeat layers and finish with a drizzle of honey on top.

Table Setup and Decor:
Use bright, cheerful tableware and fresh flowers as a centerpiece.

Serving Utensils/Glass:
A dessert spoon for a delightful scoop & a nice clear glass to show off the layers.

Garnishes:
Feel free to top it off with a sprig of mint and berries.

Inner Reflection

1. What layers do I need to cultivate in my own relationships?

2. Describe a time when you embraced the complexity of a relationship.

3. Reflect on how nurturing others enriches your life journey.

Picture Perfect

Add a photo of your prepared dish here and the people you shared it with!

Significance to forgiveness

Avocado toast symbolizes the nourishment of gratitude and can act as a daily reminder that small acts of appreciation foster healthier relationships.

Gratitude Avocado Toast

Personal Story

Avocado toast quickly became a go-to breakfast during my morning routines. Its simplicity reminds me that gratitude is often found in small, everyday moments, nourishing my body and spirit while fostering relationships.

Ingredients

- 1 ripe avocado
- 2 slices whole grain bread
- 1/2 cup cherry tomatoes, halved
- 1/4 cup feta cheese, crumbled
- Salt and pepper to taste

How to Make

1. Toast the whole grain bread until golden brown.
2. Mash avocado and spread generously on toast.
3. Top with cherry tomatoes, crumbled feta, salt, and pepper.

Presentation Items

Serve beautifully on a bright plate with a drizzle of olive oil.

Table Setup and Decor:

Use a simple table while scattering cherry tomatoes as decorations.

Serving Utensils:

A sharp knife for slicing the bread.

Place Settings:

A clean setup with earthy tones to evoke a homey feel.

Inner Reflection

1. What simple joys in my life am I grateful for?

2. Reflect on how nurturing relationships can manifest in everyday actions.

3. Describe a time when gratitude transformed a situation.

"I cherish the simple joys of life with gratitude, nurture my relationships through everyday acts of kindness, and transform challenges into growth through the power of forgiveness."

Picture Perfect

Add a photo of your prepared dish here and the people you shared it with!

Significance to forgiveness

Chia seed pudding embodies renewal and transformation through its ability to expand and create a nourishing meal. It symbolizes how forgiveness can also transform and fill us with vitality, reminding us that growth often takes time and patience.

Renewal Chia Seed Puddin

Personal Story

I first tried chia seed pudding at a wellnes retreat. The refreshing texture and flavor reminded me that nurturing oneself is essentic in the journey toward healing and forgiveness This pudding became a symbol of resilience teaching me to cherish the little things.

Ingredients

- 1/2 cup chia seeds
- 2 cups almond milk (or your preferred milk)
- 2 tablespoons maple syrup (or honey)
- 1 teaspoon vanilla extract
- Fresh fruit for topping (e.g., berries, bananas, kiwi)

How to Make

1. In a bowl, mix chia seeds, almond milk, maple syrup, and vanilla extract.
2. Stir well to combine, and let sit for 10 minutes.
3. Stir again to prevent clumping, cover, and refrigerate for at least 4 hours or overnight.
4. Serve in a glass topped with your choice of fresh fruit.

Serving Utensils & Presentation:

A small spoon for serving, and optional parfait glasses for an attractive display.

Table Setup and Decor:

Use simple neutral, white or pastel-colored plates to keep the focus on the pudding.

Inner Reflection

1. How can I be more patient with myself during my healing journey?

2. Reflect on ways small changes have created significant impact in your life.

3. Describe a moment when forgiveness allowed you to grow further.

Picture Perfect

Add a photo of your prepared dish here and the people you shared it with!

FORGIVENESS
Lunch

"A midday meal is a reminder to pause, nourish, and find compassion within ourselves. Just as we refuel our bodies at lunch, we can feed our spirit with forgiveness, allowing us to move forward lighter and kinder."

-Dr. Norma T. McLauchlin

Lunch

This quinoa salad signifies an array of experiences coming together to create harmony. It serves as a reminder that embracing differences can lead to a more enriching life.

Compassion Quinoa Salad

Personal Story

I discovered this quinoa salad while experimenting in the kitchen during a challenging time. The colorful ingredients encouraged me to think about how diverse experiences contribute to harmony, much like the ingredients in this salad.

Ingredients

- 1 cup quinoa, rinsed
- 2 cups vegetable broth
- 1 cup cherry tomatoes, halved
- 1 cucumber, diced
- 1/4 cup red onion, finely chopped
- 1/4 cup parsley, chopped
- Juice of 1 lemon
- 2 tablespoons olive oil
- Salt and pepper to taste

How to Make:

1. In a pot, bring vegetable broth to a boil. Add quinoa, cover, and simmer for 15 minutes until cooked.
2. In a large bowl, mix cooked quinoa, tomatoes, cucumber, onion, and parsley.
3. Drizzle with lemon juice and olive oil, then season with salt and pepper.

Presentation Items:

Serve in a large wooden bowl for a rustic touch.

Table Setup and Decor:

Use a woven table runner and small pots of herbs for decoration. A large spoon for serving the salad.

Place Settings:

Use natural fiber plates for an earthy look.

Inner Reflection

1. How do I nourish my body during busy times?

2. Reflect on a time when you showed yourself compassion.

3. Describe the importance of caring for yourself in your journey of forgiveness.

Mantra

❝ I nourish my body even in busy times, show myself compassion in every moment, and recognize that caring for myself is essential in my journey of forgiveness and healing. ❞

Picture Perfect

Add a photo of your prepared dish here and the people you shared it with!

Significance to forgiveness

These wraps symbolize the act of wrapping ourselves in compassion. They remind us that nourishing our bodies can also be an expression of self-love and care.

Forgiveness Hummus Wraps

Personal Story

During a busy work week, I would often prepare these wraps to enjoy during lunch breaks. They represent self-care and the importance of taking moments to wrap ourselves in compassion amidst our hectic lives.

Ingredients
- 1 whole grain wrap
- 1/2 cup hummus
- 1 cup mixed salad greens
- 1/2 cup roasted vegetables (zucchini, bell peppers, etc.)
- A squeeze of lemon

How to Make:
1. Spread hummus evenly over the whole grain wrap.
2. Layer with mixed greens and roasted vegetables, squeezing a bit of lemon over the top.
3. Roll the wrap tightly and slice in half to serve.

Presentation Items:
Serve wrapped in parchment paper with a toothpick to hold together.

Table Setup and Decor:
Create a colorful setup to reflect the vibrant ingredients.

Place Settings:
Casual, appealing place settings with earthy tones. A butter knife or spatula for spreading the hummus.

Inner Reflection

1. How can I work towards creating harmony in my own relationships?

2. Reflect on the diverse experiences in your life and how they shaped you.

3. Describe a time when you embraced collaboration with others.

Mantra

❝ I strive to create harmony in my relationships, honoring the diverse experiences that have shaped me, embracing collaboration, and finding deeper connection through the healing power of forgiveness. ❞

Picture Perfect

Add a photo of your prepared dish here and the people you shared it with!

Significance to forgiveness

This grilled sandwich represents comfort and warmth. It serves as a reminder of the healing power of shared meals and the positive connections that come from forgiveness and compassion.

Heartwarming Grilled Sandwich
Personal Story

This sandwich became a favorite after a particularly challenging week. Preparing it became a ritual that reminded me of the comfort of home cooked meals and the bonds we create around the table

Ingredients
- Sliced Whole Wheat Bread
- 1/2 cup assorted grilled vegetables (bell peppers, zucchini, eggplant)
- Thick Sliced Turkey (Optional
- 2 slices mozzarella cheese
- 1 tablespoon pesto
- Fresh Spinach

How to Make:
1. Preheat the grill or pan.
2. Grill vegetables until tender and slightly charred.
3. Slice the ciabatta roll and layer with grilled vegetables, mozzarella, and pesto.
4. Grill the sandwich until the cheese is melted and the roll is toasted.

Presentation Items:
Serve on a wooden cutting board alongside a small bowl of extra pesto.

Table Setup and Decor:
Natural fiber utensils for an organic feel.
Place Settings:
Casual, appealing place settings with a knife for cutting the sandwich.

Inner Reflection

1. How do I create comfort for myself and others in my life?

2. Reflect on how meals have brought unity to your relationships.

3. Describe a time you felt healed through food shared with loved ones.

❝I create comfort for myself and others, using shared meals to bring unity and healing to my relationships, and embrace forgiveness as a nourishing force that strengthens our bonds. ❞

Picture Perfect

Add a photo of your prepared dish here and the people you shared it with!

Significance to forgiveness

The Buddha bowl embodies the harmonious blending of flavors and textures, symbolizing the balance we seek in forgiveness and wellness.

Harmony Buddha Bowl

Personal Story

In my quest to eat healthier, I discovered Buddha bowls. Each ingredient told a story, and assembling them became a mindful practice of forgiveness and balance in life.

Ingredients

- 1 cup cooked brown rice
- 1/2 cup roasted chickpeas
- 1/2 avocado, sliced
- 1/2 cup steamed broccoli
- 1/2 cup shredded carrots
- Tahini dressing for drizzling

How to Make:

1. Cook brown rice as per instructions and let cool.
2. Roast chickpeas until crispy (about 20 minutes at 400°F / 204°C).
3. In a bowl, arrange rice, roasted chickpeas, avocado, broccoli, and carrots.
4. Drizzle tahini dressing over the top.

Presentation Items:

Serve in a deep bowl to showcase all the colorful ingredients.

Table Setup and Decor:

Use minimalist decor with fresh herbs to maintain focus on the food.

Serving Utensils:

A large spoon for serving.

Place Settings:

Ceramic bowls and spoons to enhance the natural feel.

Inner Reflection

1. How do I create balance in my life?

2. Reflect on a time when diverse elements came together beautifully.

3. Describe how cooking helps you maintain your well-being.

Mantra

❝ I create balance in my life by blending diverse elements with care, using cooking as a means to nourish my well-being, and embracing forgiveness to maintain harmony and inner peace. ❞

Picture Perfect

Add a photo of your prepared dish here and the people you shared it with!

This chickpea salad highlights the importance of gratitude in relationships. Sharing food from various cultures can lead to understanding, healing, and forgiveness.

Gratitude Mediterranean Chickpea Salad

Personal Story

I This Mediterranean salad was discovered while traveling; its bold flavors and combinations inspired me to explore how culinary differs can encourage gratitude among cultures while healing old wounds.

Ingredients

- 1 can chickpeas, rinsed and drained
- 1 cup diced cucumbers
- 1 cup diced tomatoes
- 1/4 cup red onion, diced
- 1/4 cup feta cheese, crumbled
- 2 tablespoons olive oil
- Juice of 1 lemon
- 1 teaspoon oregano
- Salt and pepper to taste

How to Make:

1. In a large bowl, combine chickpeas, cucumbers, tomatoes, onion, and feta.
2. Drizzle with olive oil, lemon juice, oregano, salt, and pepper. Toss well.

Presentation Items:

Serve on a colorful plate with a lemon wedge garnish.

Table Setup and Decor:

Use bright, art-inspired plates to reflect the Mediterranean vibe.

Serving Utensils:

A slotted spoon for easy serving.

Place Settings:

Bright, colorful napkins with a casual feel.

Inner Reflection

Mantra

1. How do I express gratitude in my life?

2. Reflect on a time when different cultures or backgrounds brought you joy.

3. Describe a moment of connection facilitated by food.

“ I express gratitude by celebrating the diverse cultures and backgrounds that bring joy to my life, fostering connections through shared meals, and allowing forgiveness to deepen those bonds and enrich my journey. ”

Picture Perfect

Add a photo of your prepared dish here and the people you shared it with!

FORGIVENESS

Dinner

"With each meal we nourish not only our bodies but our hearts. Through these daily moments, we are reminded to cultivate compassion and forgiveness, filling ourselves with the warmth and understanding needed to carry us forward."

-Dr. Norma T. McLauchlin

Signifigance

Bringing together flavors from around the world signifies unity. Allow this dish to bring you and your loved ones together for a hearty treat.

Preparation Tip

For best results, press the tofu for at least 15 minutes before cooking to remove excess moisture—this ensures a crispier texture when sautéed. Also, prepare all your ingredients ahead of time, as the stir-frying process is quick and requires your full attention.

Savored with love...

Unity Vegan Phad Thai

This vegan Pad Thai nourishes both body and soul with its vibrant, plant-based ingredients, promoting physical well-being and emotional balance. Sharing this flavorful dish can foster connection and create meaningful moments around the table. It is a dish that conjures warm memories.

Ingredients:

For the Sauce:

- 3 tbsp tamari or soy sauce (use tamari for gluten-free)
- 2 tbsp lime juice
- 2 tbsp maple syrup or coconut sugar
- 1 tbsp rice vinegar
- 1 tbsp peanut butter or almond butter (optional, for creaminess)
- 1 tsp sriracha or chili sauce (optional, for heat)

For the Pad Thai:

- 8 oz (225g) rice noodles
- 2 tbsp sesame oil or any neutral oil
- 1 small onion, thinly sliced
- 3 cloves garlic, minced
- 1 block (14 oz) firm tofu, pressed and cubed
- 1 cup shredded carrots
- 1 cup bean sprouts
- 1 red bell pepper, thinly sliced
- 3 green onions, sliced
- 1/4 cup roasted peanuts, crushed
- Fresh cilantro, chopped (for garnish)
- Lime wedges (for serving)

Vegan Phad Thai

Directions

Prepare the Sauce:
- In a small bowl, whisk together the tamari or soy sauce, lime juice, maple syrup, rice vinegar, peanut butter (if using), and sriracha until smooth. Set aside.

Cook the Noodles:
- Cook the rice noodles according to the package instructions. Once cooked, drain and rinse them under cold water to prevent sticking. Set aside.

Cook the Tofu:
- Heat 1 tbsp of sesame oil in a large pan or wok over medium heat. Add the cubed tofu and cook until golden brown on all sides, about 5-7 minutes. Remove tofu from the pan and set aside.

Stir-Fry the Vegetables:
- In the same pan, add the remaining 1 tbsp of oil. Add the onion and sauté for 2-3 minutes until softened. Add the garlic and cook for another minute.
- Add the shredded carrots, bell pepper, and half of the green onions. Stir-fry for about 3-4 minutes until the vegetables are tender-crisp.

Combine Everything:
- Add the cooked rice noodles and tofu back to the pan. Pour the sauce over the mixture and toss everything together until well combined and heated through, about 2-3 minutes.

Serve:
- Divide the Pad Thai into bowls. Top with bean sprouts, the remaining green onions, crushed peanuts, and fresh cilantro. Serve with lime wedges on the side.

Quote

"

One of the most defining moments of true friendship is to reconnect over a meal with an old friend as if you have never missed a day together.

"

Dr. Norma McLauchlin

Inner Reflection

1. How can I bring more intention and presence to the way I share meals with others?

2. What role does forgiveness play in my relationships, and how might it transform my connections?

3. In what ways can I use food as a tool to create understanding and build community?

Picture Perfect

Add a photo of your prepared dish here and the people you shared it with!

Significance to forgiveness

This hearty stew embodies comfort, serving as a reminder of the warmth in forgiveness as we come together to share a meal filled with love and care.

Compassion Lentil Stew

Personal Story

Lentil stew has been a staple during winter family gatherings. It warms not just the body but the heart, reminding us of the nourishment that compassion brings during difficult times.

Ingredients
- 1 cup lentils
- 2 medium carrots, diced
- 2 celery stalks, chopped
- 1 onion, chopped
- 4 cups vegetable broth
- 2 cups kale, chopped
- 1 tablespoon olive oil
- Salt and pepper to taste

How to Make:
1. In a large pot, heat olive oil. Sauté onions, carrots, and celery until softened.
2. Add lentils and vegetable broth, bringing to a boil. Reduce heat and simmer for 30 minutes.
3. Stir in kale, cooking until wilted. Season with salt and pepper.

Presentation Items:
Serve in rustic bowls, garnished with fresh herbs.

Table Setup and Decor:
Use a warm tablecloth and small candles for ambiance.

Serving Utensils:
A ladle for serving the stew.

Place Settings:
Natural, earthy plates and utensils for a homey feel.

Inner Reflection

1. How does compassion show up in my daily life?

2. Describe a situation where sharing a meal fostered connection.

3. Reflect on what you learned from past challenges and relationships.

Picture Perfect

Add a photo of your prepared dish here and the people you shared it with!

forgiveness Dinner

Significance to forgiveness

The colorful array of vegetables symbolizes diversity in relationships. Just like pasta, forgiveness requires the right mix of ingredients to create harmony and unity.

Forgiveness Pasta Primavera

Personal Story

Pasta primavera reminds me of family dinners where conversations flowed as freely as the sauce. It teaches me that, like pasta, our relationships require care and the right ingredients to thrive.

Ingredients

- 8 oz whole grain pasta
- 1 zucchini, sliced
- Brocolli
- 1 red pepper sliced
- 1 cup cherry tomatoes, halved
- 2 cloves garlic, minced
- 2 tablespoons olive oil
- 1/4 cup grated Parmesan cheese
- Salt and pepper to taste

How to Make:

1. Cook the pasta according to package directions, then drain and set aside.
2. In a large skillet, sauté garlic and vegetables in olive oil until tender.
3. Toss in cooked pasta, cheese, salt, and pepper until well combined.

Presentation Items:

Serve in an elegant pasta bowl with extra cheese sprinkled on top.

Table Setup and Decor:

Use a traditional Italian tablecloth with red and white patterns.

Serving Utensils:

A large serving spoon for pasta.

Place Settings:

Use Italian ceramics for a homey ambiance.

Inner Reflection

1. How do I express creativity in my relationships?

2. Reflect on a time when you learned something meaningful from a difference in perspective.

3. Describe how teamwork enhances understanding and forgiveness.

Picture Perfect

Add a photo of your prepared dish here and the people you shared it with!

Significance to forgiveness

Baked salmon represents the balance of flavors and the nourishment experienced through forgiveness and personal growth. It promotes the idea of savoring the moment and appreciating life's connections.

Harmony Baked Salmon

Personal Story

Cooking salmon became a cherished routine in my household, particularly during special gatherings. Its rich flavors symbolize nourishment and the importance of caring for those we love.

Ingredients

- 4 salmon fillets
- 2 tablespoons olive oil
- Juice of 1 lemon
- 2 cloves garlic, minced
- Fresh dill for garnish
- Salt and pepper to taste

How to Make:

1. Preheat the oven to 400°F (200°C). In a baking dish, arrange salmon fillets, drizzle with olive oil and lemon juice, and sprinkle with garlic, salt, and pepper.
2. Bake for 12-15 minutes until the salmon is flaky.
3. Garnish with fresh dill before serving.

Presentation Items:

Serve on a white platter with lemon wedges.

Table Setup and Decor:

Create an elegant setup with cloth napkins and candle holders.

Serving Utensils:

Use a fish spatula for serving.

Place Settings:

Classic white plates for a timeless feel.

Inner Reflection

Mantra

1. How does nurturing others enrich my life?

2. Describe a gathering where sharing food promoted healing.

3. Reflect on a moment where forgiveness allowed relationships to flourish.

" Nurturing others enriches my life, as sharing food promotes healing and forgiveness allows relationships to flourish and deepen. "

Picture Perfect
Add a photo of your prepared dish here and the people you shared it with!

Significance to forgiveness

Chickpea curry reflects the nourishment of gratitude. Each ingredient represents a layer of experience that enriches our lives, reminding us to appreciate life's journey.

Gratitude Chickpea Curry

Personal Story

This chickpea curry recipe serves as a connecting point to my travels. The flavors transport me to vibrant markets, reminding me that food narrates our experiences, fostering gratitude in every bite.

Ingredients
- 1 can chickpeas (drained)
- 1 can coconut milk
- 1 can diced tomatoes
- 1 onion, chopped
- 2 cloves garlic, minced
- 1 tablespoon curry powder
- Salt and pepper to taste
- Fresh cilantro for garnish

How to Make:
1. Sauté onions and garlic in a pot until translucent.
2. Add curry powder and chickpeas, stirring to coat.
3. Pour in coconut milk and diced tomatoes and simmer for 20-25 minutes.
4. Garnish with cilantro before serving.
5. Spoon over a bed of jasmine rice.

Presentation Items:
Serve in bowls with a slice of naan on the side.

Table Setup and Decor:
Use colorful, warm colors that evoke an Indian-inspired feel.

Serving Utensils:
A ladle for serving curry.

Place Settings:
Brightly colored plates to enhance the ambiance.

Inner Reflection

1. How does immersing myself in different cultures foster gratitude in my life?

2. Describe an experience when sharing a meal led to deeper connection and understanding.

3. Reflect on how flavors enhance the experience of forgiveness.

Picture Perfect
Add a photo of your prepared dish here and the people you shared it with!

FORGIVENESS

Desserts

"Life is sweeter when it is filled with moments of forgivness and reconnecting!"

-Dr. Norma T. McLauchlin

Serenity Berry Parfait

Personal Story

My love for this berry parfait grew during a summer spent with relatives at the beach. Preparing it became a ritual of togetherness, teaching me that sharing sweet moments can create lasting bonds.

Ingredients
- 2 cups Greek yogurt
- 1 cup granola
- 1 cup mixed berries (strawberries, blueberries, raspberries)
- Honey for drizzling

How to Make:
1. In a glass, layer Greek yogurt, granola, and mixed berries.
2. Repeat the layers and finish with a drizzle of honey on top.

Presentation Items:
Serve in clear parfait glasses to showcase the layers.

Table Setup and Decor:
Use summer-themed decor, perhaps with seashells or vibrant floral arrangements.

Serving Utensils:
A small spoon for each parfait.

Place Settings:
Use cheerful, colorful plates to evoke a sense of summer fun.

Compassion Chocolate Avocado Mousse

Personal Story

I discovered chocolate avocado mousse during a cooking class aimed at teaching healthy indulgences. The creaminess and rich flavors reminded me that forgiveness can often be sweetly surprising.

Ingredients
- 2 ripe avocados
- 1/2 cup cocoa powder
- 1/3 cup maple syrup (or honey)
- 1 teaspoon vanilla extract
- Pinch of salt

How to Make:
1. In a blender, combine ripe avocados, cocoa powder, maple syrup, vanilla extract, and salt.
2. Blend until smooth and creamy, scraping down the sides as needed.
3. Chill in the refrigerator for at least 30 minutes before serving.

Presentation Items:
Serve in an elegant pasta bowl with extra cheese sprinkled on top.

Table Setup and Decor:
Use a traditional Italian tablecloth with red and white patterns.

Place Settings:
Use Italian ceramics for a homey ambiance, or a unique little blow for that added personal touch.

The parfait illustrates the importance of layering experiences in life. Each layer represents a step in the healing and forgiveness journey, reinforcing that sweet results come from patience.

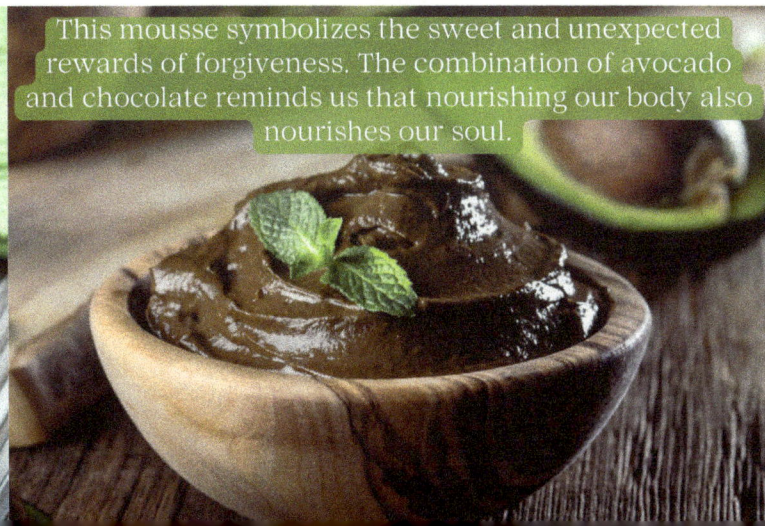

This mousse symbolizes the sweet and unexpected rewards of forgiveness. The combination of avocado and chocolate reminds us that nourishing our body also nourishes our soul.

Let's Reflect

1. How do layers of my experiences shape who I am today?'

2. Reflect on moments of joy you've shared that enrich your relationships.

3. Describe how forgiveness contributes to the sweetness of life.

Harmony Apple Crisp
Personal Story

Making apple crisp on fall evenings with my family became a cherished tradition. The warm spices and fresh apples always reminded us of the sweetness and warmth of forgiveness within our family.

Ingredients
- 4 cups sliced apples (Granny Smith or Fuji)
- 1 tablespoon lemon juice
- 3/4 cup brown sugar
- 1/2 cup rolled oats
- 1/2 cup all-purpose flour
- 1 teaspoon cinnamon
- 1/4 cup butter, melted

How to Make:
1. Preheat the oven to 350°F (175°C). Toss sliced apples with lemon juice and half the brown sugar, placing them in a baking dish.
2. In a bowl, mix the remaining sugar, oats, flour, and cinnamon. Stir in melted butter until crumbly.
3. Sprinkle the oat mixture over the apples and bake for 30-35 minutes until the topping is golden.

Presentation Items:
Serve warm in bowls with a scoop of vanilla ice cream.

Table Setup and Decor:
Use rustic dishware to evoke a cozy, home-cooked feel.

Serving Utensils:
A large spoon for serving.

Place Settings:
Mismatched vintage bowls to emphasize homey charm.

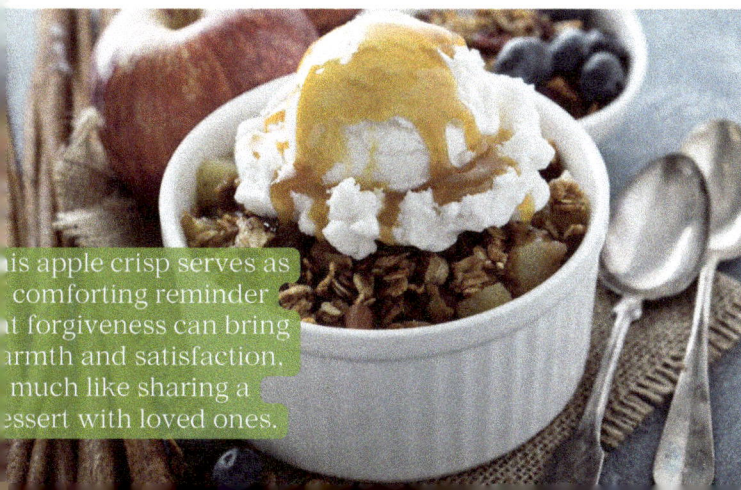

Gratitude Chia Seed Pudding
Personal Story

After attending a health seminar, I brought chia seed pudding into my morning routine. It became essential in reminding me to appreciate the small moments, cultivating gratitude on busy days.

Ingredients
- 1/2 cup chia seeds
- 2 cups almond milk (or any milk)
- 2 tablespoons maple syrup (or honey)
- 1 teaspoon vanilla extract
- Fresh fruit for topping
- Blueberry compote for layering

How to Make:
1. In a bowl, combine chia seeds, almond milk, maple syrup, and vanilla extract.
2. Stir well and let sit for 10 minutes. Stir again to prevent clumping, then cover and refrigerate overnight.
3. Before serving, top with fresh fruit.

Presentation Items:
Serve in clear jars to show the layers.

Table Setup and Decor:
Use elegant table settings with fresh fruit as decorative elements.

Serving Utensils:
A small spoon for serving.

Place Settings:
Classy, minimalist clear dishes or glasses that enhance the pudding presentation.

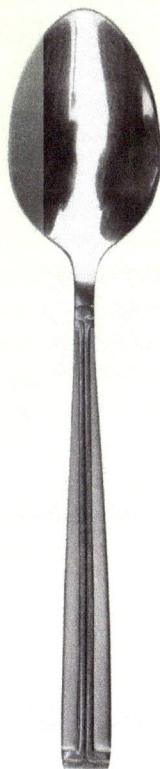

This apple crisp serves as a comforting reminder that forgiveness can bring warmth and satisfaction, much like sharing a dessert with loved ones.

The chia seed pudding embodies renewal and patience, symbolizing the importance of nurturing oneself through forgiveness. Each ingredient works together to create a healthy, fulfilling meal that reflects the beauty of slow, thoughtful processes in our lives.

Let's Reflect

1. What simple acts of self-care can I incorporate into my routine?

2. Reflect on how nurturing yourself allows you to extend kindness to others.

3. Describe a moment when patience led to a rewarding outcome.

Let's Reflect

MANTRA: Traditions bring warmth to my relationships, as sharing food fosters forgiveness and creates comforting memories that deepen our bonds.

1. What traditions have brought warmth to your relationships?

2. How can the act of sharing food foster forgiveness?

3. Describe a comforting memory tied to a shared meal.

SOOTHING SIPS

"With each sip, may peace fill your spirit, warmth soothe your soul, and calm flow through every part of you."

Dr. J. Michelle Vann

Significance to Wellness

This refreshing tea embodies tranquility, reminding us that serenity prepares us to engage in the difficult conversations surrounding forgiveness and healing.

Serenity Mint Iced Tea

Personal Story

Mint iced tea became a refreshing staple on hot days. It was during these moments of relaxation that I learned the importance of serenity in my life, allowing forgiveness to flow freely.

Ingredients

- 4 cups water
- 1/4 cup fresh mint leaves
- 4 tea bags (black or green tea)
- Honey to taste
- Ice cubes

How to Make:

1. Boil water and steep tea bags and mint leaves for 5-7 minutes.
2. Remove tea bags and stir in honey (to taste).
3. Chill in the refrigerator and serve over ice.

Presentation Items:

Serve in clear glasses with fresh mint leaves for garnish.

Table Setup and Decor:

Use cheerful colors that evoke a summer afternoon.

Serving Utensils:

A stirring spoon and a pitcher for pouring.

Place Settings:

Bright, summery plates to set a light tone.

Soothing Sips

Significance to Wellness

This turmeric latte became my go-to during chilly evenings as I found myself seeking warmth and comfort. Preparing it reminded me to nurture myself and others during the healing process.

Compassion Ginger Turmeric Latte

Personal Story

Mint iced tea became a refreshing staple on hot days. It was during these moments of relaxation that I learned the importance of serenity in my life, allowing forgiveness to flow freely.

Ingredients

- 1 cup almond milk (or your preferred milk)
- 1 tablespoon fresh ginger, grated
- 1 teaspoon turmeric powder
- 1-2 teaspoons maple syrup or honey
- A pinch of cinnamon

How to Make:

1. In a saucepan, heat almond milk with grated ginger and turmeric until warm.
2. Add maple syrup and a pinch of cinnamon; stir well.
3. Pour into a mug and serve warm.

Presentation Items:

Serve in cozy mugs, perhaps topped with a sprinkle of cinnamon.

Presentation Items:

Serve in cozy mugs, perhaps topped with a sprinkle of cinnamon.

Table Setup and Decor:

Use warm colors and comfortable settings to evoke coziness.

Serving Utensils:

A small whisk for mixing. Glassware to show off the beautiful tumeric color.

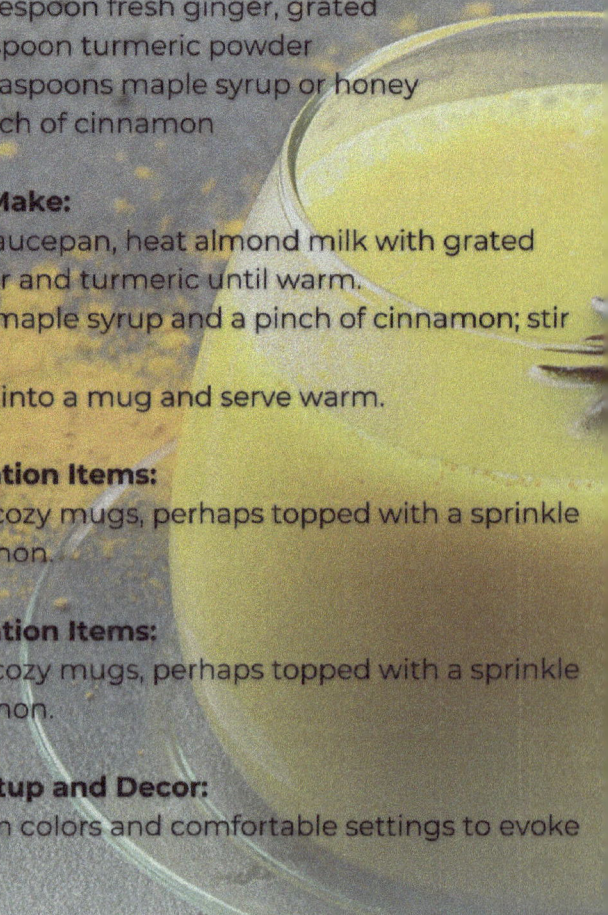

Soothing Sips

Significance to Wellness

This lavender lemonade embodies the refreshing quality of forgiveness, reminding us to embrace calm and tranquility, particularly when navigating difficult conversations and healing.

Renewal Lavendar Lemonade
Personal Story

I discovered the soothing qualities of lavender lemonade during a relaxing summer gathering with friends. The calming aroma and refreshing taste reminded me that self-care can be both enjoyable and restorative.

Ingredients

- 1 cup freshly squeezed lemon juice
- 1/2 cup honey or sugar
- 4 cups water
- 2 tablespoons dried culinary lavender
- Ice cubes for serving

How to Make:

1. In a saucepan, combine 1 cup of water and lavender, bringing to a boil. Let steep for 10 minutes, then strain.
2. In a pitcher, combine the lavender infusion, lemon juice, honey (or sugar), and the remaining water. Stir until well mixed.
3. Serve over ice in glasses.

Presentation Items:
Serve in clear glasses with fresh lemon slices for garnish.

Table Setup and Decor:
Use summer-themed decorations with fresh flowers.

Serving Utensils:
A ladle for serving lemonade.

Place Settings:
Use vibrant, summery glassware, add a sprig of lavendar and colorful straws.

Soothing Sips

Significance to Wellness

This refreshing water promotes hydration and reminds us to find gratitude in the simple pleasures of life. It encourages us to celebrate wellness in our daily routines.

Gratitude Citrus Infused Water
Personal Story

Preparing citrus-infused water has become a refreshing ritual in my household, especially during family gatherings. It reminds us to appreciate the vibrant flavors life offers and serves as a symbol of gratitude.

Ingredients

- 1 lemon, sliced
- 1 lime, sliced
- 1 orange, sliced
- Fresh mint leaves
- Water

How to Make:

1. In a pitcher, combine citrus slices and mint leaves.
2. Fill with water and refrigerate for at least an hour to let the flavors infuse.

Presentation Items:
Serve in a clear glass pitcher with slices of citrus visibly floating.

Table Setup and Decor:
Use bright, cheerful colors to reflect the freshness of the drink.

Serving Utensils:
A ladle for easy pouring.

Place Settings:
Simple, glassware to allow the citrus colors to shine through.

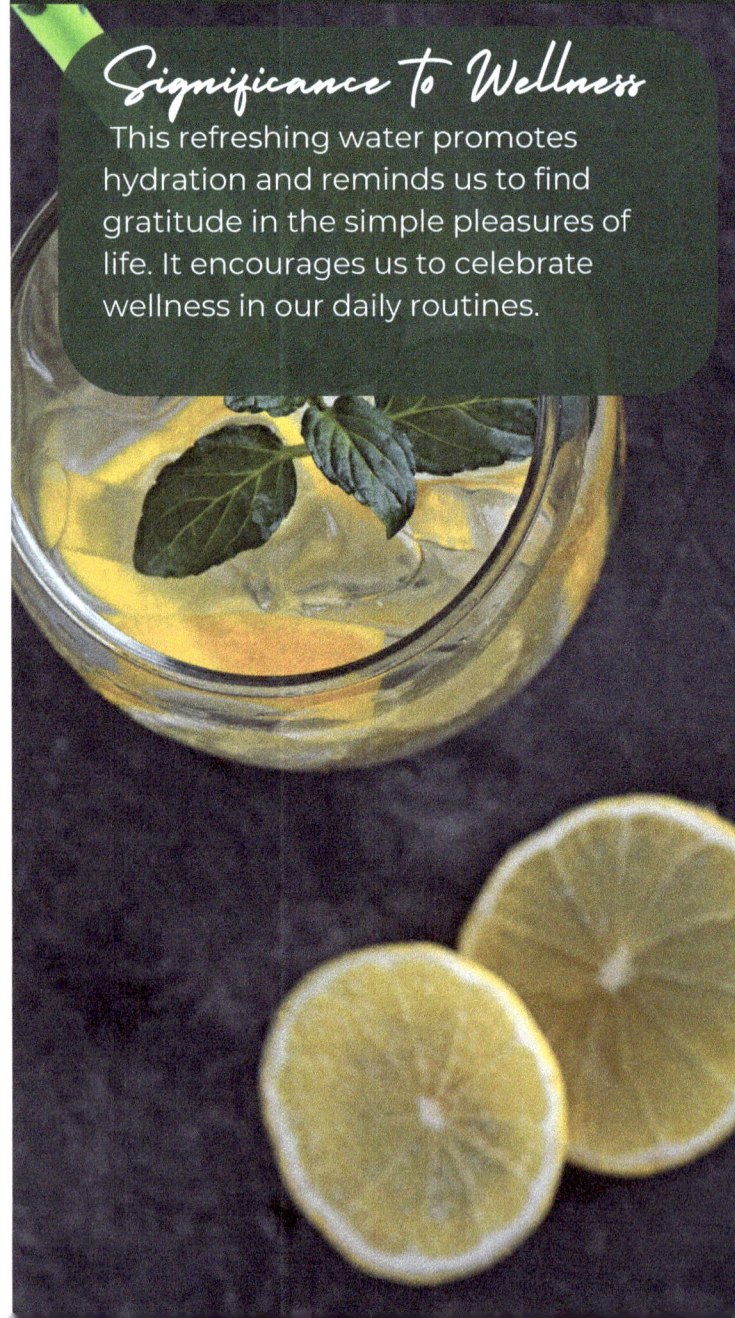

Inner Reflection

1. How do I practice self-care in my daily life?

2. Reflect on a moment when you felt comforted by nourishing food.

3. Describe how moments of warmth can facilitate forgiveness.

Mantras for Healing

1. "With each sip, I welcome healing energy into my body, releasing what no longer serves me."
2. "I drink in calm and clarity, allowing each taste to bring me closer to peace and balance."
3. "As I savor this drink, I nourish my spirit, embracing the quiet moments that lead to growth."
4. "Each sip is a reminder to slow down, reflect, and honor the journey I am on."
5. "With every refreshing sip, I renew my commitment to self-care, inviting healing with open arms."

FORGIVENESS
Snacks

"Healing begins in the small moments of forgiveness and reconnection, nourishing the soul one bite at a time."

— Dr. J. Michelle Vann

armony Veggie Sticks with Hummus
ersonal Story

eparing veggie sticks with hummus is a eloved family activity. It promotes healthy acking and allows us to discuss emotions, lping foster an environment of open mmunication and understanding.

gredients:
carrots, cut into sticks
cucumber, sliced
ed bell pepper, sliced
cup hummus

ow to Make:
Cut veggies into sticks and arrange them on a platter.
Serve with a bowl of hummus in the center for pping.

resentation Items:
erve on a colorful platter for visual appeal.

able Setup and Decor:
se fresh herbs or sprigs of vegetables as decorations for natural touch.

erving Utensils:
small spoon for serving hummus.

lace Settings:
ismatched plates to evoke a warm, homey feel.

Forgiveness Trail Mix
Personal Story

Creating trail mix has been a fun way to involve my children in the kitchen. As we mix together nuts, seeds, and dried fruits, we talk about the importance of variety in our lives and how it mirrors the journey of forgiveness.

Ingredients:
1 cup almonds
1 cup walnuts
1 cup dried cranberries
1/2 cup dark chocolate chips
1/2 cup pumpkin seeds

How to Make:
1. In a large bowl, mix together all the ingredients until well combined.
2. Portion into snack-sized bags for easy grab-and-go snacks.

Presentation Items:
Serve in mason jars or small containers to highlight the colorful ingredients.

Table Setup and Decor:
Use a nature-inspired theme with elements like twigs or wildflowers.

Serving Utensils:
A ladle or scoop for serving.

Place Settings:
Rustic fiber bowls for an eco-friendly look.

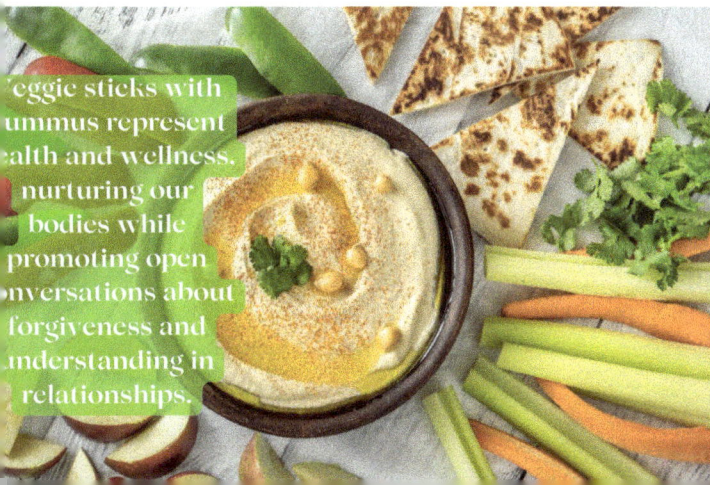

eggie sticks with ummus represent ealth and wellness. nurturing our bodies while promoting open onversations about forgiveness and nderstanding in relationships.

The chia seed pudding embodies renewal and patience, symbolizing the importance of nurturing oneself through forgiveness. Each ingredient works together to create a healthy, fulfilling meal that reflects the beauty of slow, thoughtful processes in our lives.

Gratitude Greek Yogurt Dip

Personal Story

Baking apple crisp on fall evenings with my family became a cherished tradition. The warm spices and fresh apples always reminded us of the sweetness and warmth of forgiveness within our family.

Ingredients:
1 cup Greek yogurt
2 tablespoons lemon juice
1 tablespoon olive oil
1 clove garlic, minced
1 tablespoon fresh dill (or herb of choice)
Salt and pepper to taste

How to Make:
1. In a bowl, mix Greek yogurt, lemon juice, olive oil, minced garlic, and dill.
2. Season with salt and pepper to taste.
3. Serve chilled.

Presentation Items:
Serve in a beautiful bowl garnished with a sprig of dill.

Table Setup and Decor:
Use light, airy decor with bright plates to evoke freshness.

Serving Utensils:
A small spoon for serving the dip.

Place Settings:
Serve chiled in a bowl surrounded by chilled slices of cucumber and some fresh lime or lemon with tortilla chips.

Sweet Healing Banana Bread

Personal Story

The smell of banana bread always reminds me of m grandmother's kitchen. She would bake it wheneve family gathered, filling the house with warmth. It wo her quiet way of teaching us that forgiveness an togetherness made everything sweeter.

Ingredients:
2 ripe bananas, mashed
1/2 cup Greek yogurt
1/3 cup melted butter
3/4 cup brown sugar
1 large egg
1 tsp vanilla extract
1.5 cups flour (blend all-purpose and whole wheat if desired)
1 tsp baking soda
1/4 tsp salt
1/2 tsp cinnamon
1/4 cup walnuts (optional)

How to Make
1. Preheat oven to 350°F and grease a 9x5-inch loaf pan.
2. In a bowl, mix bananas, yogurt, butter, sugar egg, and vanilla.
3. Add flour, baking soda, salt, and cinnamon, stirring just until combined. Fold in walnuts.
4. Pour into pan, bake 50-60 minutes, and let cool.

Presentation Tip:
Serve warm with fresh butter.

Inner Reflection

Mantras for Healing

1. How do healthy choices foster positive relationships in my life?

2. Reflect on a conversation that led to healing lasting impacts.

3. Describe a time when food sparked connection among family or friends.

1. Healthy choices nurture positive relationships, as meaningful conversations lead to lasting healing, and shared meals spark deep connections among family and friends.

2. Sharing food fosters connection, fills me with gratitude during meals with loved ones, and inspires me to show care and appreciation in everyday moments.

3. I honor the diversity of experiences in my life, understanding that accepting differences leads to greater insight, and embracing individuality strengthens the unity within my community.

"When we gather, we hold space for each other to release what no longer serves us."
— Dr. J. Michelle Vann

Gather & Heal
Scripts for the Heartfelt Host

Letting Go Celebration Meal
Setting the Scene
As everyone finishes their appetizers and moves to the main course, the atmosphere grows more intimate. The table is decorated with candles and flowers, creating a warm, inviting space that feels perfect for reflection.

Host: "As we settle in for this meal, let's pause for a moment to think about something each of us might want to let go of tonight. We all carry things—grudges, misunderstandings, or worries—that sometimes weigh us down. This dinner is a chance to release what we no longer need and to make space for forgiveness and peace."

Letting Go Activity
The host invites everyone to pick up the small paper and pen placed at their seat.

Host: "Take a moment to write down something you'd like to release. It could be a frustration, a past hurt, or anything you feel ready to let go of. Later, we'll have a chance to let these go together."
Everyone writes silently, placing their folded papers into a bowl as they finish.

Celebration Meal Introduction:
"This meal is more than food—it's about nourishing ourselves in a way that reminds us of the freedom that comes with forgiveness. Each dish has a little story behind it."

As everyone eats, the host encourages sharing thoughts or memories connected to the themes of forgiveness, gratitude, and compassion.

Ending the Meal with Reflection
After the meal, the host picks up the bowl containing everyone's written intentions.
Host: "Let's finish our gathering by letting these go together. One by one, if you feel comfortable, read your paper, then place it in this fire-safe bowl."

Guests take turns, each adding their paper to the bowl. The host lights the papers, watching the flames as they symbolize release.

Closing Celebration
As the evening wraps up, everyone raises a glass for a final toast.

Host: "Cheers to letting go, to embracing forgiveness, and to the love and laughter we've shared tonight."

In a world often filled with disconnection, Healing Plates: Recipes for Forgiveness and Wellness offers a unique blend of nourishing recipes and heartfelt stories that guide you toward healing and forgiveness. Dr. Norma McLauchlin intertwines the art of cooking with the profound act of letting go, reminding us that the kitchen can be a sanctuary for both the body and soul.

Through this collection, you'll discover how food can be a catalyst for connection and reflection. Each recipe is an opportunity to mend hearts, strengthen relationships, and find joy in the shared experience of a meal. Let Healing Palates inspire you to embrace the transformative power of food and the deeper connections it can foster.

About the Authors

Dr. Norma McLauchlin, founder of Norma McLauchlin Global Ministries and Chosen Pen Publishing, infuses themes of forgiveness into all her written works, guiding readers toward healing and spiritual growth. As a wife, mother, co-pastor, and educator, she connects deeply with women, empowering them through her Lady Lifers™ Women's Conferences, Bible studies, and counseling.

With a strong academic and ministerial background, Dr. McLauchlin continues to inspire transformation within her community and New Life Bible Church, where she serves alongside her husband, Pastor Allen S. McLauchlin.

Dr. J. Michelle Vann is a community servant at heart, a featured TEDx speaker and international presenter, she is an Amazon bestselling author of books that help women heal their minds, bodies, and spirits. She is the owner of Vanntastic Solutions, a wellness coaching practice, and the founder of Sistahs Can We Talk, a nonprofit working to fill gaps in health disparities among women. As an educator and wellness coach, Michelle lives by George Bernard Shaw's famous quote "Life is no 'brief candle' to me. It is a sort of splendid torch which I have got hold of for the moment, and I want to make it burn as brightly as possible before handing it on to future generations." Dr. Vann serves in her local church and various community organizations. She has been married to Dr. William Vann for 32 years, and they have two adult children.

FORGIVENESS ACROSS BORDERS

HISTORIC PHOTOS OF

OKLAHOMA LAWMEN

Turner Publishing Company
4507 Charlotte Avenue • Suite 100
Nashville, Tennessee 37209
(615) 255-2665

www.turnerpublishing.com

Historic Photos of Oklahoma Lawmen

Library of Congress Control Number: 2009933009

ISBN: 978-1-59652-559-7

ISBN: 978-1-68442-104-6 (hc)

Printed in the United States of America

10 11 12 13 14 15 16—0 9 8 7 6 5 4 3 2 1

CONTENTS

Members of the Choctaw Light Horse around 1880 include Captain Peter Conser (seated, at right) of the Moshulatubbee District. Conser's home still stands in southeastern Oklahoma near Hodgen.